SOURCES OF CULTURE
IN
THE MIDDLE WEST

SOURCES OF CULTURE
IN
THE MIDDLE WEST

Backgrounds *versus* Frontier

EDITED BY

DIXON RYAN FOX

NEW YORK

RUSSELL & RUSSELL · INC

1964

THE APPLETON–CENTURY
HISTORICAL ESSAYS

THE purpose of the series of books inaugurated with the present volume is the publication of essays of historical synthesis and interpretation rather than of fact-finding studies and detailed results of research. The series is designed to afford an attractive medium of publication for two types of historical work neither of which has hitherto been provided for adequately. The first consists of studies of especial interest which are too long for periodical articles and yet not long enough for entire volumes. The second comprises papers read on special subjects in history and the social sciences at meetings of one or other of the societies in these fields. By bringing them together in a single volume the essential unity of, and the special significance which attaches to, the papers when taken together are brought out and the larger contribution to the interpretation of the subject is emphasized.

Other volumes of the series which have been arranged for are *Democracy and Dictatorship,* by William E. Lingelbach, Robert Clarkson Brooks, and Ernest M. Patterson, and *Civilization in a Knapsack,* by Dixon Ryan Fox.

THE EDITOR

31243

CONTENTS

SOURCES OF CULTURE
IN
THE MIDDLE WEST

EDITOR'S EXPLANATION

IT is now well over forty years since Frederick J. Turner, in the most famous and most influential paper in American historiography, forged a key for the understanding of America's development. Noting the completion of primary settlement he declared that the first great chapter of American history was nearly finished, that the disappearance of the frontier meant the end of an influence and an opportunity which had given a peculiar stamp to society in this country. This enormous outlet for individual release now closing and presently to be gone, America would have to undergo a painful discipline of readjustment. His warning startled thoughtful men into apprehension as to the future of this great community. No other academic statement, indeed, had had comparable effect on this side of the Atlantic.

The escape of the ambitious poor to a more generous livelihood on wide, free land was cut off; the safety valve for restlessness and discontent was closed; the most obvious field for speculative enterprise had disappeared. At the same time that Efficiency, mechanical and administrative, de-

[3]

manded illimitable market for its product, word came that the national market was limited. Individualism, for which America had stood in the mind of the world, was challenged. Up to this time man's history—any man's history—had not seemed determined for him. Its universal subjunctive had been that it might be begun again any day he decided to move west. This promise now withdrawn, it might be necessary for him to make the best of things into which he had been born, not by mere resignation, but by taking thought,—not only his own thought, but the community's thought. In Turner's revelation were certain implications of the planned and balanced economy now recommended to the country.

But Professor Turner's prestige did not rest upon a single perception and a plausible, if disquieting, prophecy. He was an historian and concerned with the past. He advanced a thesis and, incidentally, a method. His thesis was that the moving frontier and its repercussion upon the older sections should be the central theme of American history. The method, entirely inductive once the premise had been granted, made large use of population, geographic and economic statistics, those at hand and those laboriously worked out by himself; its favorite device was the record map, so well adapted to the study of masses moving and registering various effects in a continental space. He had a Pauline faith in the truth and importance of his message and he proclaimed it with apostolic zeal and winning eloquence.

Yet the vanity and intolerance which so often mark the zealot were wholly lacking in his disposition. In his manner as in his heart there was a simple, honest friendliness that left a train of friends behind him everywhere,—that and his extraordinary interest in the work of other scholars. Perhaps a personal testimony may be pardoned: seventeen years ago the present writer, who had never studied with Turner and of whose existence the professor had doubtless never heard, took the liberty of sending him a recently published article, as young men do, in the wistful hope of contributing some mite of substance to a master's rich store. No acknowledgment was expected and the author was surprised to receive a kindly note in reply. Thus encouraged he sent along his next paper, and within a few days had back a nine-page longhand letter, setting forth not only helpful comment on that modest effort but a detailed account of the discoveries the professor himself had been making in an unrelated field, the settlement of the upland South. Such letters, very probably, are cherished in every part of the country and help explain the affectionate memory in which he is held by a great

[5]

number of American historians who never sat under his formal instruction. Hundreds such proudly claim membership in his "school." Any one of them in taking issue with a point of Turner doctrine does so with some reluctance and with all possible courtesy and respect. To his seminal idea and his compelling rhetoric must be added his magnetic and friendly personality in explaining why the American Historical Association and similar Sanhedrins in the social studies became, as one irreverent wag has put it, "One Big Turner Verein." But to overstress the qualities of his heart would wrong his mind; his host of disciples are followers chiefly by conviction.

As might be expected the most ardent champions of Professor Turner's orthodoxy are his own students and those who live and work in the West. To the history of westernism he added not only knowledge but dignity; from it, he maintained, had flowed the potent and flavorous essence of America. Previous standard historians, for the most part, had neglected the influence of westernism,—not argued against it, but neglected it, largely through ignorance. To the highly civilized region which still calls itself the West, neglect seemed more cruel than attack, and in the voluminous writings of the Turner school—they have been

[6]

among the most productive as well as among the ablest American historians of recent times—one detects a note of vindication. In fact, some have been as romantically loyal in combating what they thought unseemly indifference as were James K. Paulding, Timothy Dwight, C. J. Ingersoll, and Robert Walsh a little more than a hundred years ago against the aspersion of Sydney Smith on American history itself.

It was not unnatural that some students of American culture should come to fear that the balance was being upset. They were very willing, of course, to concede that the frontier influence gave America many of its peculiarities and accounts for many differences that mark off its society from those of Europe. They were willing even to admit that to some future historian who reviews a thousand years of institutional development "the similarity of institutions" might seem "less important than their differences." But they believed it gave a distorted picture of American cultural history to concentrate upon its differences from other cultural history. It was fairly obvious, they thought, that American civilization conformed generally to the pattern of Western Christendom, especially that of Northern Europe. Without denying the repercussion of frontier influence upon the older

[7]

sections they sought to discover the technique of the direct percussion made by metropolitan influence upon the newer sections.

A few years ago a paper entitled "Civilization in Transit" was read before the American Historical Association; it is now published in a companion volume. No presumptuous comparison with Professor Turner's argument was intended. He was largely concerned with primary settlement and the psychosis that resulted from it and affected the national temper. The essay referred to, not an answer but a supplement, was designed to suggest how pioneer society was itself changed, not only by its own autochthonous evolution but by the constant flow of social devices, particularly specialized competence, from the more mature communities to the eastward.

As the West was colonized from the East, it seemed clear to the writer that the western settlements were and naturally had to be for a long time cultural colonies of the older homelands. Admitted that they invented parts of their culture to fit their environmental need, they took from the East, where they already existed, higher and higher arts and practices as fast as they were able to support them. It would have been impossibly foolish to have waited to invent all the higher culture they needed when it was at hand not far away and indeed was frequently offered at their doors. Being intelligent, they continuously adopted ideas and institutions which flourished in the older East. The trouble with this observation is its obviousness; but the technique of transfer was not obvious, and, it was thought, this invited careful and systematic study. Indeed, it was feared that the Turner school in emphasizing the original had taken the derivative for granted, if they had not overlooked it, and it was urged that efforts be made to redress the balance.

The paper mentioned repeated the familiar dictum that "the West" in American history refers to a moving marginal area and that as the whole movement went forward Wests were constantly transforming themselves, or being transformed, into Easts. But the writer desired to emphasize that the West should be considered vertically as well as horizontally, that in the scale of civilization when a West had become East with respect to one layer it was still West with respect to a higher layer, that a region might be East in agriculture and still West in sculpture. There emerge successive pioneers as one considers different layers. Much is said of the West's borrowing culture, as if, having by careful judgment determined that it could use a certain competence, it deliberately reached into the East and took it. This it often did.

[9]

More often culture was not brought on order but taken on risk. Some culture, or civilization, was sent, forwarded by organized missionary impulse, especially in the case of religion, but most of it was carried by pioneering quite as individualistic as that of the first settlement. It was heroic pioneering too, for many a pioneer of culture was despised and rejected in the new country. The risk-taker had made too rosy a guess as to his welcome. Times were not ready for him and he perished.

"Civilization in Transit" was not sufficient in substance and not sufficiently controversial in tone to provoke formal rejoinders. But its author was brought to realize that his thesis, or rather his emphasis, was not universally accepted. As a member of the program committee for 1933 he suggested that the subject of Western culture, particularly its sources, be taken up at a special session of the annual meeting. It is a notorious defect of such meetings that the papers too frequently lack philosophic breadth, that the program consists too exclusively of tiny monographs of narrative information little calculated to stir reflective thinking. Quite as important and unfortunate is the fact that too seldom the program even at a single session reveals an integrating idea; if by chance it does, the idea is seldom a proposition to which the participants can bring different points of view and contend,—in other words, a proposition that is discussable. Several sessions were therefore planned in the hope of restoring to the gathering of a learned society some of that atmosphere of friendly contention more common in the nineteenth century than in our own, when intensive specialization has distracted attention from large human problems, and to create a lively partisan interest more associated with our colleague social studies of economics and government than with that of history. The origins of culture in the Middle West, it seemed, afforded an excellent subject for such a session, and the present editor was commissioned to arrange it.

A brilliant young Easterner, who had already flung a challenge against the Turner thesis in general, was asked to consider it with particular reference to political ideas and constitutional schemes. On the other hand three distinguished Turnerians were summoned to discuss the alleged cultural debt of the West to the East, though it was suspected that they would recognize it only at a heavy discount. The result was a thoroughly enjoyable and profitable evening. Here and there was the desired spice of controversy, as when one participant cited an article by another "for confusion on this point." When one speaker declared that the transforming influence of the frontier "as it appears in Turner's essays is largely myth" and that his thesis was "narrow and provincial," many faces in the audience reddened with resentment. Important exceptions were taken, it will be noted, to the chairman's own argument in his "Civilization in Transit." If lively interest was the objective, the session was a success. Moreover, each participant supported his contentions with such ample, fresh and probative evidence as to remove the discussion from the realms of thin verbosity and airy speculation into which theories and counter-theories so often wander. It was not surprising that a wide demand immediately expressed itself that the papers be printed in a volume of their own.

The chairman-editor, seizing this opportunity of rebuttal, may say that he still believes that the technique of transfer affords a promising phase, perhaps the most promising phase, of the study of Western culture. Those who would minimize it must assume that the first pioneers held within themselves nearly all the seeds of the high civilization, in its material, intellectual and moral aspects, which the Middle West now undoubtedly enjoys. That does not seem plausible, despite Professor Craven's identification of Audubon and

Dr. McDowell as typical early Westerners. Professor Hicks makes the point, readily admitted, that the Middle West had largely completed its provincial period before the end of the nineteenth century and that in some respects it was by then instructing the East, as in its substitution of government control for *laissez faire* with respect to business monopolies. But that merely means that the process of adoption and the achievement of maturity sped more rapidly than some have realized, and that certain contributions were indigenous to the West, growing out of its conditions. Both he and Professor Hansen remind us that some European ideas landed in the West and spread to the eastward, but that seems only an eccentricity in the great movement of ideas from the Old World to the New. It is pointed out that litterateurs like Mark Twain, Howells, and Garland arose in the West; but it will be noted that they arose and came out of it to flourish in the East, where they could be supported. He is merely claiming too early a date for independence; in the twentieth century they might have stayed at home sure of applause substantially expressed in income.

There is no disposition here to carp at small differences or with irenic benevolence to pretend that differences do not exist. Usually a valuable paper raises more questions than it answers. Certainly

[13]

the four here presented will stimulate useful inquiry on many lines. The fact that they are all cogently designed and competently written will make them delightful reading, no less at the merchant's fireside than on the seminar student's table.

POLITICAL INSTITUTIONS AND THE
FRONTIER

BENJAMIN F. WRIGHT, JR.

IN this essay on the early development of political systems in the Middle West I have two objectives. I desire, first, to trace some of the principal lines of institutional growth because of their significance in the constitutional history of the United States. That portion of our history is much more than the story of the national constitution and its interpretation. In any political society, and particularly in one organized on the federal principle, the development of local institutions is an essential part of the entire pattern; in some respects and at certain periods it is of more consequence in the lives of the citizens of the country than the changes which may be taking place in the central structure. The westward migration of constitutional customs surely deserves a more careful analytical and comparative study than it has yet received. Second, I wish to use the material brought together for this purpose as a point of departure from which to appraise the interpretation of American history first propounded by Frederick Jackson Turner forty years ago. The most brilliant and the most influential of American historians, Turner, has colored all of our thinking about the growth of the American nation. His striking generalizations have been repeated countless times, but they have never been subjected either to the analysis or to the tests which the rudiments of scientific method would seem to suggest. A picture of the movement of political institutions is not one of sufficient scope to make possible a complete consideration of so inclusive a thesis. Indeed the whole canvas of American history is inadequate for the purpose; one must in addition take into account many aspects of Canadian, Latin American, and European history. But if a complete re-examination is neither possible nor intended here a partial consideration may at least suggest the principal points of strength and of weakness in the frontier approach.

In dealing with the constitutional beginnings of the Middle West I shall concern myself not with the very earliest political society of that region but with its institutions when they are first embodied in written constitutions and relatively settled laws. There are, aside from limits of space, three reasons for doing so. In the first place, the earliest institutions, so far as they were sufficiently established to be dignified with that name, were frequently temporary expedients designed to serve a temporary purpose. They were intended for the period in which of necessity the pioneers concentrated upon essentials. In the second place, the settlers of the territorial period were not entirely free agents. The Ordinance for the Northwest Territory was one of the most liberal statutes ever enacted for the government of a territory, but it did determine many aspects of early political activity. Finally, and most important, is the reason that the real test of the frontier period's influence is not the history of that short period but the history of what resulted when the pioneers left it behind and adopted for themselves institutions of their own choosing. It is here that we have the opportunity to estimate the results of the period of primitive existence through which the frontiersmen had lived.

So far as I have been able to determine, there was no considerable desire among those who framed the early western constitutions to introduce governmental forms different from those long well established in the East. In all of the states of the Middle West the familiar pattern was adopted,—a single executive, a bicameral legislature, and a hierarchy of courts. The only exception to this system in any new state was Vermont, and its unicameral legislative system was a direct copy of that contained in the Pennsylvania constitution of 1776. The abandonment of this provision in 1836 brought to an end an experiment which might have had considerable value.

In local government the story is much the same, excepting that here there were somewhat greater variations among the sections of the East. The result, in general, was a parallel westward movement of local institutions. To be sure, the scattered character of western settlement, together with the artificial township boundaries of that area, prevented the settlers from New England from establishing a thoroughgoing New England town system, but otherwise there is no important exception to the principle of westward extension of local forms. In Ohio, for example, a county-township system upon the Pennsylvania model was established, and subsequently copied in Indiana. Michigan, probably because of a relatively larger migration from New York following the opening of the Erie Canal, adopted the township-county system of that state, one in which the township played a somewhat greater rôle in local affairs and in which the county board was composed of township supervisors. This was later copied in Wisconsin. In early Illinois, because of heavy immigration from the South, the county was of more importance than in other states of the section. As the northern part of the state grew in population and influence, the desire for the township system developed. In consequence the constitution of 1848 made that form, on the New York-Michigan model, optional, and it was subsequently adopted in most of the northern counties while those in the southern part of the state continued under the former system.

As urban areas developed in these states, the forms of municipal government found in the older states were introduced. Even the cumbersome bicameral municipal council crossed the Alleghenies and found a home (fortunately temporary) in the new cities.

Probably the most characteristic political idea of the American people is distrust of elected officers, legislative and executive. Certainly in this country we have hedged their powers about more carefully than has any other democracy. This distrust is manifested in the detailed character of our constitutions, in the difficulty of amending them, in the principle of separation of powers with its correlative, checks and balances, and in judicial review of legislative and executive actions.

So far as concerns the length and scope of their constitutions, the middle western states differed not at all from contemporaneous eastern models. During the Revolution the tendency was toward longer and more detailed documents, as a comparison of

the Massachusetts constitution of 1780 with those
adopted in 1776 will show. That tendency has continued to our own time. The Illinois constitution of
1848, for example, is over twice as long as that of
1818. And although there is perfectly definite evidence in the earlier document of something less
than complete trust in the legislature and governor,
that distrust had grown to such an extent by 1848
that many questions earlier left to be determined
by those departments were now regulated by constitutional provision.

In six of the Revolutionary constitutions there
was a distributing clause, that is, a clause stating
the separation of powers principle, and specifying
that it should be observed in the government established under that constitution. In most of those
documents there was, by later standards, little separation between legislature and governor. But it is
evident that there was a strong tendency in that
direction, as the New York constitution of 1777,
in which the governor was made elective by the
people rather than by the legislature, and the
Massachusetts constitution of 1780 indicate. The
second constitutions of New Hampshire (1784),
Pennsylvania (1790), and Delaware (1792) reflect
the strength of this tendency. It was the lead of
these states which was followed in the Old Northwest. And in all of the early constitutions of this

region save those of Ohio and Wisconsin, there was a distributing clause. In those states the national constitution, which separates even its statement of the separation principle, was the model.

Ohio, in its first constitution, followed the example of most of the Revolutionary constitutions in giving to the governor no veto. Illinois first adopted the New York system of bestowing this power upon a council of revision, made up of the governor and certain of the judges. All of the other states adopted a variant of the executive veto which had previously been adopted in Massachusetts, in the national constitution and in the second or third constitutions of a number of eastern states. In one respect, however, most of them followed the lead of Kentucky. In the first constitution of that state the Massachusetts-national system according to which the executive veto could be overridden by a two-thirds vote of both houses was adopted, but in its second constitution (1799) it reduced the vote required to a majority of the total membership of both houses. The popularity of this system in the West would seem to indicate that the governor was not so generally hailed as the trusted man of the people as has sometimes been supposed. Its later abandonment by all except one or two of the states indicates that it was not to be an innovation of lasting importance.

[21]

The item veto, one of the most powerful weapons the governor now has, was first introduced by New Jersey in 1844 and was subsequently copied in many western constitutions.

Judicial review is a conservative device which no other country in the world has imitated, excepting to the extent that the courts serve as referee between central governments and member states in a number of federal systems. It developed here in the colonial and early constitutional periods out of a variety of circumstances and ideas. So far as I have been able to determine no American constitution has made provision for it, but during the late eighteenth and early nineteenth centuries its use became general, in the West as in the East.

What has been said about the structure and relative powers of the departments of government applies with equal force to the tenure of office. In the original constitutions there was a strong tendency toward annual elections, but there was also very considerable variation. The western states ordinarily chose neither the briefest nor the longest tenures, although sometimes they did both in the same constitution, but were somewhere between the extremes. In general, there is no indication in this regard of any genuine difference between the opinions of contemporaneous constitution makers, in the older and in the newer states.

There remain to be considered those institutions which have an even more direct bearing than do the ones thus far considered upon the extent to which the political society of this section reflected a desire for a broader distribution of power and privilege, that is, for greater democracy.

The pioneers took over, without question, the device of a written constitution as the expressed will of the people. They further imitated one or another of the plans for the preparation, adoption, and amendment of such documents. When the Massachusetts convention in 1778 submitted to the voters a proposed constitution it was inaugurating the democratic method which was, sooner or later, to be followed by almost every state in the union. The method provided for the revision of the constitution in that state, by a convention elected for the purpose after the voters had expressed their desire for such action, or that adopted in Maryland in 1776, a favorable vote in two successive legislatures, was the pattern followed in all of the western states.

All of the early western constitutions, furthermore, contained bills of rights. The models here were, of course, the Revolutionary constitutions, certain provisions of the Ordinance for the Northwest Territory, and the relevant parts of the Constitution of the United States. The new states occasionally made a few additions to the conventional list of reserved rights, but, without exception, they represented no genuine change in political ideals or constitutional practice.

Perhaps the most frequent claim made for the democratizing influence of the pioneer period is the lead taken by the states which passed through this phase during the late eighteenth and early nineteenth centuries in securing a broader suffrage. That these new states did help to accelerate a process under way before they were settled is clear. But it is equally clear that they did not attempt, or even desire, to carry that process beyond the goal previously attained in several of the older states. The broadening of the suffrage really began during the Revolution when five states measurably reduced the amount of the property required. One state, Pennsylvania, went beyond this and imposed no property requirement other than the payment of some public tax. By 1792 four other states, South Carolina, New Hampshire, Georgia, and Delaware, had followed Pennsylvania's example. Two of these, New Hampshire and Georgia, abandoned even the tax qualification by 1798, but when Ohio entered the union in 1802 her constitution contained that limitation. It was not until 1816, when Indiana became a state, that any state in what is now the Middle West went further than had

Pennsylvania in 1776, and by that time not only New Hampshire and Georgia, but also Maryland and South Carolina, had dropped both property and tax qualifications. Indiana and the other states of this section which followed her example were not blazing a new trail; they were proceeding along one clearly marked for them by the more advanced states of the East. They showed no intention of pushing that path further. Indeed, all of them excluded free Negroes, although New York and five of the New England states admitted them to the suffrage right.

The influence of the newer states upon the reduction of the qualifications for the holding of legislative and executive offices is similar to, but probably greater than, their influence upon the suffrage. In nearly all of the older states property qualifications for office holding continued into the nineteenth century. In a few of them religious qualifications are also to be found. That these limitations would not long have survived the forces that had for decades, perhaps for centuries, been at work in the eastern part of the United States and in the western part of Europe is hardly to be questioned. Nevertheless it does seem to be clear that the newer western states, which, excepting for two or three in the lower Mississippi area, adopted neither property nor religious qualifications upon

[25]

office holding, helped to speed up the process of democratizing that part of the constitutional system.

We have frequently been told that it was the pioneer regions in such states as Virginia and South Carolina which struggled for and finally secured something approximating representation on a population basis in the legislatures. One could wish for a more inclusive account here, for in many states, especially in New England, the process is almost reversed. Long before any western state was admitted to the union we find in eastern constitutions the statement of the principle of representation according to population. Vested interests in those states sometimes prevented the application of this rule with complete impartiality. In the earlier period it was usually the thinly settled areas which were discriminated against, but later it was the rural sections which, in states east and west, prevented the cities from having their proportionate share of representatives. One of the most striking examples of this is the long refusal of the Illinois legislature to redistribute seats in that body so that Cook County might be represented in accordance with its increased population.

In the number of executive and judicial officers elected by popular vote the influence of the western states is more definitely to be seen. As I have previously pointed out, there was during the last quarter of the eighteenth century a marked tendency toward the elective governorship. The same tendency is found in the case of the lieutenant-governorship and in that of the total membership of the legislatures. The older states provided, however, that the other state executive and judicial officers, excepting for some holding positions of local jurisdiction, should be appointed by the governor or by the legislature. In all of the constitutions adopted in the Middle West before 1848 the example of the eastern states is followed. There were relatively few new constitutions adopted in the East during the first half of the nineteenth century, but in those the practice of popular election for officers other than the governor and the legislators made slow headway. Connecticut in 1818 did provide for popular election of a treasurer and secretary, but this was exceptional. The first state to adopt a constitution requiring the election of virtually all of the judicial and executive officers of the state was Mississippi, which did so not in its first constitution of 1817, but in the second constitution which came fifteen years later. The example of this state was not followed by Michigan when it framed its first constitution in 1835, nor by Iowa in 1846, but after the acceptance of the general elective principle by Illinois and Wisconsin

more democratic practices where there was variation in the East, but even in this respect they never
varied from some well established seaboard model,
unless it was in the case of the proportion of elected
officials. And even in this instance, which came not
directly from the pioneering period but after a
considerable interval had elapsed, one can trace
precedents and some tendencies in this direction
in the older states. In short, the result of the developments in the newer section seems to have been
somewhat to accelerate the rate of growth of the
democratic movement, not to change its direction.

It will be remembered that in his original essay
on the influence of the frontier Turner wrote in
the crusading mood of one who battles for a dear
and a long neglected cause. It was with vigor and
enthusiasm that "he hitched his star to a covered
wagon." His conclusions begin with his first paragraph and they lack not in inclusiveness. "The existence of an area of free land, its continuous
recession, and the advance of American settlement
westward, explain American development. . . .
The true point of view in the history of this nation
is not the Atlantic coast, it is the Great West." [1]*
Like most historians of his time he believed individualistic American democracy to be the fine

* See the end of the essay for this and other references.

[29]

flower of modern civilization. And it, along with the other characteristic features of American life, could be accounted for only by reference to the frontier.[2] The principal arguments supporting this conclusion seem to be the democratic character of pioneer life, the effect of free land upon the discontented and the ambitious and the opposition of the frontiersmen to unjust control by the dwellers in the eastern communities. In many essays written during the next ten years the changes are rung on these early assertions. And the cynic who said that "history may not repeat itself but historians repeat each other" was something of a prophet so far as Turner's numerous followers are concerned. Reiteration of Turner's generalizations, or, more often, the implicit assumption of their truth, has been their scholarly method of testifying to his influence. I have elsewhere argued that the frontier interpretation is inadequate, even seriously misleading, as an explanation for the growth of American democracy.[3] I wish here merely to consider the applicability of one part of this body of doctrine to the early constitutional development of the Middle West.

In an article published in 1896 and dealing with the attempts at state-making by the Westerners during the Revolution, this statement appears in the conclusions: "the frontier modified older forms

tions of American democracy? The frontier era was ordinarily one of short duration. If my interpretation of the data is correct, those who had lived through such a time were at least as desirous of establishing political and legal systems on the eastern model as they had been when they moved to the frontier. Of course, since most of them were men who, in the older states, were among the under-privileged, they usually desired to adopt the constitutional devices which gave to more persons a share in political power. But as they showed no desire to tinker with the institution of property or to allow their legislatures to pass laws violating the sanctity of contracts, so too they did not extend political powers to women or to Negroes. I may perhaps add that my own observations of the institutional life of a state removed by only a few decades from the time of the frontiersmen strengthen my belief that the conception of the "transforming influence" of the frontier, as it appears in Turner's essays, is largely a myth. Indeed, I believe that a much better argument can be made out that the hardships of pioneer living transformed a large proportion of the restless and discontented who migrated to the free and promised lands into men ambitious to be prosperous citizens in the image of the bankers and merchants and landowners back home. If this thesis isn't always applicable to some

[32]

of the wilder and farther West, it is eminently so to the Middle West.

That reference to some of the differences between various "Wests" gives an opportunity to introduce a penultimate observation. The so-called frontier interpretation was never simply that. Among other things it was, from the beginning, a sectional interpretation of American history.[7] A glance at the titles, as well as an analysis of the content in *The Frontier in American History* indicates as much. Furthermore, it is in good part a Middle West-sectional interpretation. A devoted citizen of that region, Turner almost invariably had its history and its characteristics in mind when he generalized about the West or the frontier. Consequently an analysis of the influence of the frontier upon the political development of the Middle West is particularly favorable to the Turner thesis. In the South West, for example, slavery was not the only undemocratic institution carried from the old to the new lands. And if I could choose for my point of reference the Great Salt Lake Basin it would be easy to prove that frontier life transformed those who had lived under a comparatively individualistic and democratic system into the loyal adherents of oligarchy and paternalism. Doubtless it also accounts for the change from monogamy to polygamy.

[33]

There is one final, possibly fatal, challenge to deal with. The usual answer to any criticism of Turner's doctrine is about this: "Turner never said what you make him say. You have only set up a man of straw and then proceeded to demolish him." I think that the difficulty of interpretation here is largely due to the two-fold character of Turner's work. He was both a remarkably able investigator of relatively detailed points of historical scholarship and a poet who wrote in the grand manner. As a teacher he was cautious in the extreme. His acuteness as a researcher was equaled by his hesitancy in formulating broad conclusions. But in his poetic capacity he wrote brilliant and moving odes to the glories of the westward movement. In 1893 he stated his propositions not as hypothesis but as thesis. During the next twenty-five years he published the twelve essays included along with the original one in the *Frontier* volume. They contain elaborations of the original doctrine, but they do not contain qualifications nor any expression of doubt as to the complete truth of the original declarations. The statements from his writings which I quoted were wrested from the context and doubtless they appear somewhat less extreme when read in the light of the complete argument. But such statements are made and repeated so frequently that they are not exceptional, and certainly they are never qualified. Some of the most romantic passages appear in essays written toward the close of Turner's career. Consider, for example, the well-known paragraph in the essay published in 1914, twenty-one years after the first essay appeared: "American democracy was born of no theorist's dream; it was not carried in the *Susan Constant* to Virginia nor in the *Mayflower* to Plymouth. It came out of the American forest, and it gained new strength each time it touched a new frontier. Not the constitution, but free land and an abundance of natural resources open to a fit people, made the democratic type of society in America for three centuries while it occupied its empire." [8]

As an exhortation to the faithful, a colorful declaration of American independence from European ideas and practices, and a fine tribute to those of our ancestors who carved for us homes and security out of the wilderness, it is a splendid piece of writing. But, unfortunately, it is more misleading than it is helpful. Let us consider it briefly.

If any one ever said that American democracy was the product of a single theorist's dreams, or, for that matter, the product of the entire residuum of political speculation, he probably was not taken very seriously. Obviously no theorist or group of theorists dreamed into existence the queer patchwork of institutions that we call American democracy. But what is gained, except misunderstanding, by an ungracious exclusion of Locke and Milton and Montesquieu, of Coke and Blackstone and Grotius, of Adams, Jefferson, Otis, Paine, and Madison from a share of the credit? One has but to compare the differences between the institutions of the English and those of the French, Dutch, and Spanish colonies in America to see that the foundations, and more, of our democracy were brought in the *Susan Constant* and *Mayflower*. That democracy did not come out of the American forest unless it was first carried there. On some frontiers democracy was not strengthened, rather the reverse. Free land gave the opportunity to establish slavery in Louisiana, oligarchy in the Mormon state, the hacienda system in Mexican California, while it was furnishing the opportunity for a "fit" people in the Middle West to establish the particular degree and kind of democracy that they favored.

If Turner's thesis had not been so widely relied upon, there would be no point at this late date in subjecting his generalizations to critical analysis. Certainly I have no desire to disparage his standing as an historian nor to minimize the stimulating effect that his writings had upon the American historiography of the last generation. He did have the genius to see in certain neglected factors extraordinarily useful instruments. If, in his zeal for his cause, he over-stated his case, that was more than pardonable, it was probably necessary. But the desirability of unquestioning acceptance of his sweeping doctrine vanished long ago. His thesis has, like previous interpretations, served its purpose. Continued reliance upon his unclarified and unmodified doctrine is more an indication of imaginative poverty than of loyalty to a dead leader. It has been many times said that each generation must reinterpret history to suit its own preconceptions. If we to-day find Turner's thesis of forty years ago to have been narrow and provincial, to have emphasized unduly the characteristics peculiar to some sections and some frontiers, to have elevated to the stature of universal principles values which are beginning to be found something less than perfect, we are simply doing for our time what he did for his. And the longer such an attitude is postponed, the more likely is it that instead of critical appraisal, which would mean the retention of the still useful portions of Turner's thesis as well as the discarding of those found to have outlived their time, we shall have uncompromising attack in which the destruction might be spectacular but the salvage negligible.

THE ADVANCE OF CIVILIZATION INTO THE MIDDLE WEST IN THE PERIOD OF SETTLEMENT

AVERY CRAVEN

THE occupation of new areas by the American pioneer was but the first step in an extended process. The rugged frontiersman pushing his way through the forest and over the plains was beginning a transformation which would end logically in cities and factories, intensive farming and far-flung exchange. He was the advance agent of an effort which would exploit the riches of the wilderness and replace it with that complexity called "civilization." He was one with the men of Western Europe, who, with growing capital and an expanding technology, had already widened the avenues of commerce and ushered in the Industrial Revolution. From rude, isolated beginnings, American life has ever been hurrying forward to busy marts and crowding factories which somehow tie the interests of mankind strangely together.

Progressive change drew the distinction between "the frontier," "the New West," "the Old West," and "the first hives" from which both men and

[39]

ideas began their swarming, and yet made the varied experiences of each a part of a single great national and international epoch. To understand this fact is to fit the lone axman or cowboy into his proper relationship with trusts, depressions, and international congresses. With equal emphasis on crude frontier beginnings and the final achievement of a mature society American history reaches its proper balance. When viewed as a social process it becomes a chapter in human experience. By such an interpretation Frederick Jackson Turner lifted the story of simple, scattered localities, engaged in the homely tasks of living and living better, into the dignity of world history. By it he not only gave complete unity to the American story, but he wove it into the story of mankind, both past and present.[1]

The settlement of the American West was, therefore, not an isolated movement. The characteristics developed there were not entirely unique. Pioneering dominated the age. Change was in the air. Behind frontiers older regions altered their ways to the growing forms of modern industrial society. While the latest West was "beginning over again," older Wests, now become Easts, went "forward with civilization" by achieving more advanced stages in a common pattern. Technical improvements and constantly reordered economic-social groupings, thrust forward by the new age, rendered their social orders almost as fluid as did the presence of free land render that of the West. Opportunity for new talents and new ways enabled submerged groups to acquire those things on which privilege had been established, and sent waves of democracy rolling forward. The New England country boy who turned cityward in the 1830's found places as unfilled, and ways of commerce and industry as unfixed, as his brothers found them in the West. It is no denial of the democratizing influence of the frontier to point out the fact that both Europe and older America showed a like development. Opportunity, whether from lands or machines, broke the crust which age had developed. Civilization was in transit the western world over, and democracy was a part of that "civilization." [2]

The peculiar thing about the rôle played in this process by any American West was its elemental character. To enter constantly a region occupied only by Indians and wild life meant a return to primitive social-economic conditions. The steady westward drift of individuals and scattered families produced a long, wavering region where men were scarce and nature abundant—or, if you wish, where society was atomized. The lone settler was stripped of the accumulations which living with others gives and forced to become a self-sufficing

[41]

agent, supplying his wants from what his environment afforded. His standards, fixed in an older society, had to yield almost completely for the time being. Primal needs for food, shelter, and clothing had to take precedence, and the skill of his own hand and the cunning of his own brain had to measure the degree of comfort he enjoyed. All of civilization which group living makes possible in division and specialization of labor, co-operative institutions, and accumulated capital had yet to be acquired. Most of what has been called "culture" lay even farther ahead. The real need was for neighbors. The addition of plain hands for physical tasks meant a gain well beyond the actual increase of man power. A social increment was secured. In no other way could nature be exploited and her riches carried to profitable markets. In no other way could skilled services and complex institutions be developed.

Under the pressure to keep alive and make "progress," the frontiersman often violently altered the pattern of life brought from the older regions. New ways and means, better suited to the immediate requirements of time and place, were invented. Often he took whatever lay nearest at hand in reality or memory and fitted it to his needs. He was both evolving and borrowing his civilization.

This reshaping of practices and institutions has

been called "Americanization," simply because the original patterns with which the American began were European in origin.³ But such a labeling should not obscure the fact that the great majority of first settlers were largely attempting to hurry through the period of intense privation to that "better life" which they had known in other days and which was fundamentally European in structure. Nor should it imply that the older regions were less "American." The West had no monopoly on adjusting old forms to new needs in a period when the whole western world was moving out toward a new order which had its beginnings and greatest advance in England itself.

In the Ohio Valley, embracing portions of Pennsylvania, Ohio, and Kentucky, as well as a long, narrow wedge running across southern Indiana and Illinois into Missouri, we have something of a unit which constituted the first Middle West. Beyond it and above it, ever a stage behind in development to 1860, lay a second region, embracing the remainder of the Old Northwest and parts of Iowa and Minnesota. Together they formed a giant section equal in area to the original thirteen states or to pre-war Germany and Austria-Hungary combined. Its geographic form was relatively simple, but varied enough to present three distinct zones. To the south, the lands along both sides of the Ohio River, covered with hardwoods and partly untouched by the later glaciers, formed something of a unit. To the north, the Great Lakes Basin, with its dense pine forests shading southward into hardwoods and oak clearings, constituted a second zone. Between them and blending into each, the prairies widened and swept off to the west.

The section throughout was well fitted to agriculture of the corn and live-stock variety. The northern and central portions formed also a potential wheat belt of great richness, and the Kentucky lands on the extreme south quickly proved their value for hemp and tobacco. Mineral deposits existed in several localities. The pine forests along the upper lakes were the richest yet encountered by the American pioneer. The Ohio and Mississippi river systems and the Great Lakes, soon to be supplemented by the Erie Canal, offered natural highways to the outside world on the south and the east. Nature had done her part well.

After early French and English days and up to 1860, three main streams of population entered this Middle West. From the upland South came the first settlers to occupy the Ohio River valley, where the abundance of wood and water satisfied their requirements. Largely English, Scotch-Irish, and German in blood, but well mixed by years of

[44]

moving and toiling in the Piedmont region, they blended without discord with the steady flow which soon set in from the lower Middle States. Sallow, lean woodsmen they were as a rule, with homely vices and virtues and with more than their share of half-starved emotions—men who without show or complaint set about reproducing the life they had known in such varied places as tidewater Virginia, back Pennsylvania, and the upper Carolinas. In spite of substantial islands of New England and foreign settlement, they gave flavor to the entire region until the middle of the 1830's and brought it to a stage which men in upper Illinois of that day called "finished."

The second stream of population, caught and held for a time in upper New York, swept along the lakes and into the northern hardwood and prairie sections in the decades after 1830. They were New England and New York born, carrying with them the economic and social patterns of those regions. They broke the prairie soils, added a bit more of professional service than was common to their neighbors, and soon began exploiting the northern forests as they had already done their own.

The third element came from abroad. Englishmen and Germans had early entered the Ohio Valley, but in the '40's and after, a new flow set in from

Germany, Ireland, and Canada to give a decidedly foreign tinge to portions of the Lake-Prairie region and to deepen the flavor in Cincinnati and eastern Missouri. By 1850 there were over 640,000 foreign-born in the North Central region. Coming into a land where institutions, habits, and values were as yet unfixed, they found it much more a "mixing-bowl" than a "melting pot,"—a place where divergent elements could adjust themselves by compromises into a comfortable civilization. The Irishman, toiling on canal or railroad at first, ultimately found a place in the rising towns or on farms along the transportation lines he had helped to build. The plain German took up the poorer lands, often in heavily wooded corners, or accepted the opportunities afforded in the towns to become butcher, baker, or candlestick maker. The more cultivated Forty-eighter found larger opportunity, but only in rare cases did he secure a following outside the bounds of his own people. Lesser groups from other foreign countries sought lands for farming and were forerunners of the days yet ahead, rather than immediate factors in the shaping of society.

Such was the stage and such the people who by 1860 had advanced civilization in the Middle West from wilderness conditions to those well along the path set by the Industrial Revolution. Concretely

and thereby emphasize the advancing character of civilization. The first, extending roughly to 1825 in the Ohio Valley, and to 1845 in the Lake-Prairie region, might be designated as the "home market period." It began with scattered self-sufficing individuals or families and advanced to an agricultural surplus sold to new arrivals or walked or floated to distant centers. "We can always sell all the produce we raise . . . to travellers like you and other newcomers," said the Ohio Valley farmer to the foreign visitor in 1818, and then explained that "cattle and pigs, which can travel to market somewhere," would take care of the rest.[4]

It was a meager and uncertain condition, never yielding returns large enough to lift the standard high, and profitless enough to give rise to periods of provincialism in which resentments ran sharply against the older societies for controlling markets or for dominating government. Some urged the diversification of the economic life of the West to the point of complete independence. Some, in anger, advocated political action which would force a more satisfactory condition. The West in the War of 1812 can better be understood as a section thwarted in its struggle for satisfactory markets and lodging the blame for failure against Great Britain, rather than as a region bent on expansion or drunk with patriotism. Governor Huntington's de-

mand in 1810 that Ohio import artisans, not finished goods, aimed not only at a more dependable
supply of necessities but at the building up of "a
market for the production of our soil" as well.
Even the Jacksonian Democracy of the next decades was much more the expression of Western
resentments than it was a devotion to abstract principles.[5]

The second period, coming after 1825 in the
Ohio Valley and after 1840 in the Lake-Prairie
zone, was one in which the home market "broke"
and economic readjustments were necessary. Thousands, unable to make the changes required, sought
new homes in the farther West, or forsook agriculture for new endeavors in the neighboring towns.
Each region, in turn, entered upon the task of fit-
ting its life into the larger national pattern and
finding those economic efforts for which it was
especially fitted. After a period of uncertainty and
suffering, progress was rapid. Larger co-operative
activity resulted in the building of canals and railroads which reached new markets. Agriculture
was diversified and specialized. Manufacturing of
national consequence developed. Banking hurried
out of the "wildcat" stage to new soundness, and
outside capital sought investment within the region. The Ohio Valley was ready for Henry Clay
and his American System in the 1830's and '40's,

and the Prairies were turning with equal enthusiasm to the Republican Party and its Whiggish
economic program in the 1850's.[6]

In this period in each zone, the cities grew at
an astonishing rate. In the Ohio Valley, Cincinnati outstripped her old rival, Lexington, and became the "Queen of the West." Capitalizing on
the great corn and live-stock area about her, she
became the "porkopolis of the nation." Distilling
and brewing, and the manufacturing of machinery, furniture, and clothing, added to a growing
commerce which now went north and east as well
as south and west. St. Louis, Cleveland, Columbus,
and dozens of smaller towns grew at equal pace.
The Valley was acquiring that concentration of
population so essential to social progress.[7]

Chicago played the part of Cincinnati in the
Prairie developments of the next generation when
the kingdom of wheat spread westward. In 1850
she had a population of under thirty thousand; ten
years later it was over one hundred and nine thousand. Her industry and commerce expanded in
proportion, and the placing of street lights and the
development of a water system testified to her public spirit. Detroit, Milwaukee, and Toledo all
quickened their pace, and even towns like Springfield began passing ordinances requiring that pigs

running in the streets should wear rings in their noses.[8]

The Middle West was thus making material progress which implied the advance of civilization and the larger opportunity for culture. At this level, it is impossible to draw a line between the two aspects of a single development. Johnny Appleseed or William Woodbridge, bringing fruit trees to the region, was as much the agent of civilization as was John Scull or John Bradford, who published the first books.[9] The rude blacksmith or miller was more essential to advancement in the first days than was the teacher or the preacher. It was in accord with sound principles that the first successful public efforts were toward the building of internal improvements rather than the establishment of art galleries and libraries. A water system might evidence cultural advancement. Material and spiritual things possessed a strange unity in the early Middle West.

It is, however, possible to gain some idea of the ways in which things not entirely material were secured. Both the pressure of past experiences in older sections and the cruel necessities of the wilderness dictated the early addition of both persons and institutions which administered to higher needs. The assertion that the settlers "planned and acted only in reference to security from the arm of justice, the acquisition of wealth, or the means of animal subsistence," and that "temporal things . . . [were] more powerful and controlling," was only part of the truth.[10] They might accept ill health as part of the common lot and the epidemic as a visitation from heaven, but they retained a faith in the powers of medicine and those who dared to administer it. The patient hunter sitting on a stump waiting for the "shakes" to pass so that he might shoot a squirrel, was counterbalanced by the riders who rushed into the villages, during the cholera epidemic, calling for "The Doctor! The Doctor!"[11]

The restless settler might "squat" on government lands and administer a rough-and-ready justice on occasion, but he did relish the security which the mysterious papers drawn by a lawyer gave him to the possession of his homestead and the more regular justice dealt out by a court. The Illinois legislature, in 1835, was responsive to the taunting question: "Shall Illinois, with its unrivalled location, beauty, fertility, and natural resources, which prepare it to stand preëminently in the Confederacy, degrade itself in the eyes of the whole nation by refusing to foster literary institutions?"[12] It was Peter Cartwright who threatened to send western missionaries back to New England in answer to the charges that Illinois was barbarous and uninterested in the things of the spirit.[13]

Even before population could give permanent support, the doctor, the lawyer, the teacher, and the clergyman made their appearance. Where group migrations took place, one or more of these specialists often accompanied the settlers. More often they came alone under the urge for adventure or the desire to serve. Their quality was both high and low, sometimes equal to the best of the day; more often, hardly deserving the name "professional." That magnificent group of "intelligentsia" at New Harmony, including world-famed educators, scientists, and artists, was as normal ı part of the West as was that Illinois legislator who boasted that he had not been spoiled by "book larnin'." It was a period which might well be called "the chance stage of civilization,"—one which might offer a drifting John James Audubon or a Dr. Ephraim McDowell along with its mass of ordinary people.[14] It corresponded, in rough fashion, to the home-market period in economic affairs, and it passed, as such periods have passed the world over, with the growth of towns and the spread of commerce into wider fields. Concentration of population alone enabled qualified specialists in all lines to gain permanent foot-hold and to organize for the elimination of the charlatan and for providing easier access to efficient training.

In the first period of "chance," the physicians who serve the Middle West were both abundant and varied in ability. Many were army surgeons, who found time from post duties to aid the civilians.[15] Most were average men driven by the spirit of adventure or the pressure of justice or public opinion. The good Dr. Goforth, mobbed in New York for dissecting a human body, found refuge in Cincinnati in 1800, there to condemn the accepted practice of bleeding and to preach the benefits of vaccination.[16] Young Daniel Brainard, fresh from the College of Physicians and Surgeons Medical School in western New York and with post-graduate work at Jefferson College in Philadelphia, went to Chicago in 1835, soon to realize his ambition in the founding of Rush Medical School.[17] Dr. Baty, receiving fourth honors at the Medical School in Paris and thereby entitled to a place on its staff, preferred to locate in Vincennes, Indiana, in 1835.[18] And to these should be added Daniel Drake and Benjamin Dudley, who, reared in the West but educated in the East and Europe, turned back to the Ohio Valley to practice and teach with rarest skill. Associated with such men as Samuel Brown and Charles Caldwell, they made Transylvania Medical School, as well as other institutions later established, equal in quality to those of the older sections.[19]

Alongside these, and far more typical, were such men as Dr. Burr, "The Root-Doctor," of Connorsville, Indiana, who imparted all his knowledge to students in three weeks and granted them diplomas to practice,[20] or the one described by Faux, who made a "poor Englishman a cripple for life" by his lack of skill in setting a broken leg.[21] Most of the earlier physicians had to supplement their practice, even though it ranged over hundreds of miles, by farming or politics, and many moved about constantly in search of patients. Even the specialists were jacks-of-all-trades in the early Middle West.

The lawyers and teachers of this period were of the same sort. Men who had "read law" in some older community were on the ground early enough to be disliked for the little formality they represented, and at a time when business was so scarce that they were forced to become land agents or politicians. John Reynolds described those he knew as "sound headed and respectable men, who had no pretension of law learning." [22] But there were others, like Miles Eggleston of William and Mary,

Jacob Burnet of Princeton, Vincent Bradford of Philadelphia, or men of the rugged Stephen A. Douglas type, who might have been weakened by formal training.[23] The states generally required admission to practice by a license from the court or a number of judges, but this seems to have been a form inherited from the older states rather than a requirement for standards.[24]

The teacher was often the first specialist in the West. Regardless of origins, the western American had a deep faith in education as the guardian of democracy. Even in the unglaciated portions of the Ohio Valley, where illiteracy was appallingly high, the teacher was welcomed whether he were "a cross, ill-natured Irishman" or "an aged and respectable pioneer." Aided by federal land grants, the states generally made provision for school systems but failed to put their legislation into operation.[25] Here, as in other things, the early schools were, in quantity and quality, a matter of chance, and the final work of improvement was the result of professional organization. In regions where the southern and middle state population dominated, the schools were as brief and as poor as those described by John Mason Peck or John Reynolds, but were leavened here and there by a schoolroom or academy under the guidance of a born teacher.[26] The regions settled by New Eng-

landers presented a better situation. The act of
1827 in Michigan, building on the work of
Father Richard, John Monteith, and Mr. Dan-
forth, provided for schools of varying standards
in the townships, according to population, and
soon a complete state system, the third in the
United States, ranging from elementary school to
university, was in operation under the guidance
of John D. Pierce of New Hampshire and Brown
University. Wisconsin, with such leaders as Mi-
chael Frank and such towns as Kenosha and Ra-
cine, achieved the tax-supported school and the
free state university well before the first provincial stage in things economic had ended.[27]

In higher education the influence of church and
eastern missionary groups somewhat altered the
process. Yet the chance abilities of individual
leaders largely determined the quality of the
dozen or more colleges established before 1829,
and the thirty-odd ones added by 1850. Transylvania, at Lexington, Kentucky, founded in 1798
by western evangelical zeal and eastern donations,
rose and fell in quality with her presidents, reach-
ing a climax under the Rev. Horace Holley of
Yale. When the trustees, to use the words of a
local periodical, were forced to choose between
Jesus Christ and Holley, the college declined at
once.[28] New England groups in Ohio, with the

SOURCES OF CULTURE IN THE MIDDLE WEST

founding of Ohio University, Miami, and Western Reserve, adopted a course of turning back to
their native section for men and funds, and pre-
pared the way for the establishment and development of a whole series of middle western schools.
The Yale Band at Illinois College and the Society
for Promotion of College and Theological Education at the West, which gave aid to Western Reserve, Oberlin, Illinois, Wabash, Marietta, Lane,
Knox, Wittenberg, and Beloit, were the fullest expression of this movement but not its entirety. New
England men played an important part in founding the universities of Michigan and Wisconsin,
and even in Indiana, where the Methodists, Bap-
tists, and Christians were painfully erecting
colleges, they took a hand in evolving a state university.[29] The Middle West was borrowing "civilization" from those who thought, with the pious
Philander Chase, that it was worth the while "to
raise up men to minister to the flock of Christ in
the remote West."

The newspaper advanced into the Middle West
well ahead of the region's ability to give permanent support. Land-Office and government print-
ing often sustained these simple sheets, which
lived solely for political ends. All led a checkered
career amid the difficulties of securing supplies,
obtaining news from a limited and uncertain ex-

change list, and accepting subscriptions in produce which ranged from dried apples to cordwood. They took color and quality entirely from the abilities of the editors, who, in the early period, were generally printers, or, as one writer charged, "quack doctors, half-read lawyers and pretended literary characters [who] had invaded the field." Their influence, too often, depended upon the capacity of the editor to inflict and absorb physical violence.[30]

Of the subscription libraries which sprang up occasionally among men with better backgrounds, and faded as material problems increased, only mention can be made.[31] They were akin to such early literary magazines as *The Medley* and the *Western Review,* both of Lexington, James Hall's *Illinois Magazine* and the *Cincinnati Literary Gazette,* whose quick death, like that of the others, furnished, as the editor said, "one more instance of the futility of all hopes founded on the anticipated encouragement of those intellectual exertions which contribute to soften and adorn life among a people whose highest ambition would seem to be exhausted in acquiring the means of support." [32] The chance artist, who, like William West, Asa Park, or "Mr." Beck, found opportunity to paint an occasional portrait or a panel of "fruit and flowers," probably does not deserve

notice, but he does indicate the existence of trans-
planted tastes which in time might support greater
talents.[33]

The clergyman was early on this "western
front." The church was generally the first social
institution erected. To an unusual degree both represented the urge within eastern men and organizations to carry light into darkened corners.
Under its drive Catholic priests and Protestant
circuit riders followed the crowding edge of settlement to check the inherent bent to moral individualism and to impose established patterns on a
forming society. The call to service fell sometimes
on those well fitted to minister to exacting tastes.
More often it came to those only a trifle in advance
of frontier mental and spiritual levels. Many only
added church rivalries and emotional conflicts—
often mistakenly called "clash of creeds" to the
already turbulent spirit of the West. Yet a
Peter Cartwright, a John Strange, or a John Mason Peck more than righted the balance.[34] If one
here and there, like the Reverend Orson Parker
of Flint, Michigan, would throw his delinquent
parishioners into the street in order to collect
his salary, the great majority were more like
Luke Williams of Missouri, who tended his own
"truck-patch and corn fields" and took "nary a
cent" from the many churches he served.[35] But re-

gardless of the quality of those who preached, their churches formed the center about which the social structure arose, the one place of intellectual stimulation for adults, the one point of emotional outlet. No other agents did so much for midwestern civilization.

The developments under the second economic stage, coming with the towns and supported by commerce and industry of national import, need only be briefly summarized. They represented the gradual growth of civilization as contrasted with the chance borrowing of the earlier day. In medicine, the better-trained physicians, now able to organize and bring pressure on public opinion, largely eliminated the quack and developed the local medical school to furnish adequate training. At Transylvania, where the department had barely survived, new growth began in the 1820's. Kentucky secured a second medical school at Louisville in 1836, and Ohio, with its first in 1832, added eight more schools by 1850. Indiana and Illinois, meanwhile, acquired at least seven, and only the inflow of well-trained eastern doctors kept the number down in Michigan and Wisconsin.[36]

In like fashion the local and state bar associations lifted standards in the legal profession, and a law department became a necessity at each of the new state universities and at many of the smaller colleges. The teachers in the public schools also organized to give something of reality to the early promises in public education. In Ohio, "The Western Literary Institute and College of Professional Teachers," formed in 1831, made a beginning with the Stowe Report of 1837 towards a real state system. In the next decade, Horace Mann, at Antioch College, found opportunity to put his ideas on coeducation, non-sectarianism, and teacher training into practice. A step behind in Illinois, the State Educational Society, backed by the brilliant J. B. Turner, forced the establishment of a State Normal School and the appointment of a State Superintendent of Public Instruction as the basis for a tax-supported school system. Indiana fell behind when the courts nullified the 1850 constitutional provisions for public schools, but individual towns went ahead unchecked.[37]

Progress in higher education was marked by the broadening of instruction, the employment of a larger number of western professors and a larger dependence on local support. In 1858, after a campaign for funds, President Sturtevant of Illinois College declared the results "incredible." "Illinois College dwells among its own people," he wrote. *"It is at home."* By 1850 there was one college student to every 2,800 people in the North Central region.[38]

Western newspapers, meanwhile, reached maturity. In all the larger cities dailies—national in news outlook and metropolitan in influence—existed. Eastern papers circulated more widely after 1840, but the names of Halsted, Prentice, Storey, Sulgrove, Penn, and Blair rivaled that of Greeley in their respective localities. The smaller papers also prospered, and there were over 500 weeklies in the section in 1850, averaging from one to each 8,400 persons in Michigan to one for each 10,400 in Indiana.[39]

Cincinnati in this era became a publishing center of real importance, providing not only the famous Eclectic school texts by the hundreds of thousands, but also books and periodicals of every description. Literary magazines, with longer life spans, printed the verse and prose of western writers. Ranging from the *Western Messenger,* which has been rightly called "A Boston Flower blooming in the Ohio Valley," to Gallagher's *Hesperian,* Hine's *Western Literary Journal,* and Hall's *Western Monthly Magazine,* they showed an increasing western bent. Few persons made a profession of writing, but the Cary sisters, Harriet Beecher Stowe, Helen Tuesdell, Albert Pike,

[63]

Coates Kinney, Morgan Neville, and even Salmon P. Chase and William O. Butler paid serious attention to the art without being entirely discredited.[40]

Painting and sculpture also gave livelihood to a growing number. Lexington, where an inherited weakness for family portraits had long been sparingly indulged, now gave creditable support to Jouett, Bush, Frazer, and Morgan. Joel T. Hart found there both the inspiration and the opportunity to become a sculptor, and, although he turned eastward for training and production, his greatest works found their way back to his native state.[41] Cincinnati, with an art hall and picture gallery, boasted of some twenty artists of varying talents, and of as many more who had left her for greater opportunities elsewhere. Chicago, which in 1850 viewed paintings occasionally brought in from the outside, by 1859 "could plan a formal art exhibition" and give serious consideration to the plans of her greatest artist, G. P. A. Healy, for a free art gallery. The Muses had discovered "Transappalachia." [42]

The concert tours of famous musicians crept westward with the new eras. Singing societies and musical associations of various kinds increased the quantity and quality of their efforts. Cincinnati and St. Louis led the way, but Chicago in the '50's boasted "a full orchestra," a Philharmonic Society, and a season of grand opera.[43] Even in the smaller communities, especially where the German element was strong, the time and taste for better music were found. As one native expressed it: "When German social habits were no longer considered of the low, sordid, animal kind, both his beer and his Beethoven gained in favor."

Religious leaders and institutions changed less than did these other things. The circuit rider, with a firm conviction that men had lost in fiber and institutions in fervor, gave way to the resident clergyman as population concentrated. The imported "educated preacher" was now supplemented by the graduates of local denominational colleges and theological departments. The evangelical groups still predominated. The Catholic church grew with immigration but lost ground comparatively. Unitarian and Universalist churches secured footholds in a few scattered corners where rational thinking on religious problems carried less of stigma than in the days of the frontier "unbeliever." But emotional upheavals and theological conflicts still persisted. Social movements still relied upon the church to give moral impulse and furnish the organized support necessary. For the average man the church remained the center of social and intellectual interests. It gave a conservative touch to an otherwise unsteady order.

Complexity and interdependence had thus arrived. First processes had already long since passed into regions nearer the setting sun. The Middle West, thinking like William H. Seward and Amos Lawrence, was "civilized" enough to want larger cities, bigger factories, and more wealthy men. Soon it was ready to join in the fight to death against the agricultural South as the embodiment of all that was anathema to American life and a larger civilization. It had played one small part in a drama, the plot of which had been written long ago, and which had been played over and over again on other stages. But western men, ever a bit provincial, believed their accomplishments were original and different, local and immediate.

[1] See not only *The Frontier in American History,* but also *The United States, 1830–1850: The Nation and Its Sections,* and *Encyclopædia Britannica,* XXVII, 733–735.

[2] See *Yale Review,* N.S., XX, 349–365, regarding confusion on this point.

[3] Professor F. J. Turner used the term in this way. For misunderstanding of the term, see *Pacific Historical Review,* II, 33–51.

[4] Thwaites, *Early Western Travels,* XI, 204, 233–234;

S. J. Buck, *Illinois in 1818*, pp. 129–130; H. C. Hockett, *Western Influence on Political Parties*, pp. 91–112; Joseph Schafer, *Agriculture in Wisconsin*, p. 130; *Wisconsin Hist. Collections*, XIII, 326–327.

[5] Beverley W. Bond, Jr., *The Civilization of the Old Northwest*, pp. 406–415; E. A. Riley, *The Development of Chicago . . . as a Manufacturing Center Prior to 1880*, pp. 25–43; G. R. Taylor, "Prices in the Mississippi Valley Preceding the War of 1812," *Journal of Economic and Business History*, III, 148–163; Thomas P. Abernethy, "Andrew Jackson and the Rise of Southwestern Democracy," *Am. Hist. Rev.*, XXXIII, 64–77.

[6] G. S. Callander, "State Enterprise and Corporations," *Quarterly Journal of Economics*, XIII, 111 ff.; *The Journal of Business of the University of Chicago*, IV, 68–90; *Niles' Register*, Sept. 27, 1834, Aug. 18, 1838; I. D. Andrews, *Trade and Commerce upon the Great Lakes and Rivers*, p. 175; R. E. Chaddock, *Ohio before 1850*; *Transactions of Illinois State Agricultural Society*, VIII, 225; J. G. Thompson, *Rise and Decline of Wheat Growing in Wisconsin*; Logan Esarey, *History of Indiana*; T. C. Pease, *The Frontier State*.

[7] Charles Cist, *Cincinnati in 1851*; W. F. Gephart, *Transportation and Industrial Development of the Middle West*; *De Bow's Review* (Old Series), VI, 431 ff.; *Indiana Magazine of History*, XXII, 245–270.

[8] E. A. Riley, *The Development of Chicago and Vicinity as a Manufacturing Center Prior to 1880*, pp. 44–133; A. C. Cole, *The Era of the Civil War*; A. T. Andreas, *History of Chicago*, I; Logan Esarey, *History of Indiana*; Joseph Schafer, *Four Wisconsin Counties*; G. N. Fuller, *Economic and Social Beginnings of Michigan*.

[9] *Michigan Pioneer Collections*, X, 69–74; H. Chapin, *Adventures of Johnny Appleseed and His Time*; W. H. Venable, *Beginnings of Literary Culture in the Ohio Valley*, pp. 36–57; W. H. Perrin, *The Pioneer Press of Kentucky*, Filson Club Publications, Number 3.

[10] *Home Missionary,* March, 1835, p. 183; April, 1840, p. 272; Feb., 1829, p. 168.

[11] *Indiana Magazine of History,* X, pp. 285–288; C. H. Rammelkamp, *Illinois College,* pp. 58–61.

[12] C. H. Rammelkamp, *Illinois College,* pp. 65–67.

[13] *Autobiography of Peter Cartwright,* pp. 359–360.

[14] Audubon, the artist and ornithologist, was in the West most of the time from 1810 to 1826. Dr. McDowell, a graduate of the University of Edinburgh and a pioneer in abdominal surgery, lived in Danville, Kentucky.

[15] G. W. H. Kemper, *A Medical History of the State of Indiana,* pp. 5–7, 69; Irving S. Cutter, "Dr. John Gale, a Pioneer Army Surgeon," *Ill. State Hist. Soc. Journal,* XXIII, 630–641; John H. Hanberg, "U. S. Army Surgeons at Fort Armstrong," *ibid.,* XXIV, 609–629; L. H. Zeuch, *History of Medical Practice in Illinois,* pp. 20–75.

[16] W. H. Venable, *Beginnings of Literary Culture in the Ohio Valley,* p. 302.

[17] L. H. Zeuch, *History of Medical Practice in Illinois,* pp. 162–210. Dr. J. C. Goodhue, of Berkshire Medical College and Yale, was Brainard's associate in securing a charter. The faculty at first was composed entirely of Eastern-trained men.

[18] G. W. H. Kemper, *A Medical History of the State of Indiana,* p. 8.

[19] Otto Juettner, "Rise of Medical Colleges in the Ohio Valley," *Ohio Archaeological and Historical Quarterly,* XXII, 481; E. D. Mansfield, *Life and Services of Daniel Drake, M.D.;* Robert Peter, *Medical Department of Transylvania University,* Filson Club Publications, Number 20; Robert Peter, *Transylvania University, Its Origin, Rise, Decline and Fall,* Filson Club Publications, Number 11. Mention might also be made of such men as Frederick Ridgely of Transylvania, William Beaumont of St. Louis, J. V. Z. Blaney of Chicago and the Illinois College group of Prince, Adams, Jones and Stahl.

[20] *Indiana Magazine of History,* X, 285–288.

[21] R. G. Thwaites, *Western Travels*, XI, 235–236 [Faux's Journal].

[22] *My Own Times*, pp. 66–67.

[23] *Indiana Magazine of History*, VII, 243; *Dictionary of American Biography*, III, 294; *Michigan Pioneer Collections*, XVII, 391, 405; III, 131–139, 429; *Wisconsin Magazine of History*, I, 270, n.; II, 392–412; V, 329–347; *Ill. State Hist. Soc. Journal*, VI, 335–336; XII, 127–128.

[24] E. A. Miller, "History of Educational Legislation in Ohio," *Ohio Arch. and Hist. Soc. Pub.*, XXVII, 116; *Statutes of Illinois*, 1858, pp. 675–676.

[25] *Indiana Magazine of History*, IX, 91; XII, 193–213; *Ohio Arch. and Hist. Soc. Pub.*, VI, 35–58; John Reynolds, *My Own Times*, pp. 58–60; E. D. Jones, "Educational Pathfinders in Illinois," *Ill. State Hist. Soc. Journal*, XXIV, 1–4; XII, 264–270.

[26] The influence of the Quaker groups in Indiana deserves notice. See: Harlow Lindley, "The Quakers in the Old Northwest," *Miss. Valley Hist. Ass'n Proceedings*, V, 69–72; *Ohio Arch. and Hist. Soc. Publications*, XXV, 40; A. K. de Blois, *The Pioneer School*, p. 22.

[27] K. F. Geiser, "New England and the Western Reserve," *Miss. Valley Hist. Ass'n Proceedings*, VI, 62–78; *Michigan Pioneer Collections*, V, 184–187, 547–550; VII, 36–51; *Wisconsin Hist. Collections*, V, 321–346; XIV, 48–62 [first kindergarten in the United States]; IX, 27–46; Joseph Schafer, *Four Wisconsin Counties*, pp. 194–247.

[28] Robert Peter, *Transylvania University, Its Origin, Rise, Decline and Fall*, Filson Club Publications, Number 11; J. H. Townsend, "Horace Holley, LL.D: Third President of Old Transylvania," *Miss. Valley Hist. Ass'n Proceedings*, VIII, 123–134.

[29] Chas. F. Thwing, *A History of Higher Education in America*, pp. 213–235; Society for the Promotion of Collegiate and Theological Education at the West, *Annual Reports*, 1844–1848; C. H. Rammelkamp, *Illinois College*, pp. 2–93;

Indiana Magazine of History, IX, 218–19 [Indiana University]; *Michigan Pioneer Collections,* XIV, 329; IV, 27–42; B. R. Hall, *The New Purchase;* Joseph Schafer, *Four Wisconsin Counties,* pp. 248–258; T. A. Wylie, *Indiana University, its History, 1820–1890;* R. G. Boone, *History of Education in Indiana.*

[30] *Indiana Magazine of History,* XXII, 297–333; II, 121–126; V. C. Stump, "Early Newspapers in Cincinnati," *Ohio Arch. and Hist. Soc. Pub.,* XXXIV, 169–183; *Illinois State Hist. Soc. Journal,* XXIV, 5–7; XXIII, 371–439; *Wis. Mag. of History,* I, 269, n.; VII, 459–472; VIII, 171–180; III, 392–393; VI, 136–149; *Michigan Pioneer Collections,* XIII, 489–490; XVII, 369–380; XVIII, 382–397; X, 515–533.

[31] W. H. Venable, *Beginnings of Literary Culture in the Ohio Valley,* pp. 129–160, 254–264; *Ohio Arch. and Hist. Quarterly,* XXI, 462–465; XXVII, 134–137; XXVI, 58–77 [Coonskin Library]; *Ill. State Hist. Soc. Journal,* VI, 246–251; *Indiana Magazine of History,* XXVIII, 240–246; XIX, 209–212; *Wis. Hist. Collections,* III, 506.

[32] W. H. Venable, *op. cit.,* pp. 58–123, 267–298; "Literary Periodicals of the Ohio Valley," *Ohio Arch. and Hist. Soc. Quarterly,* I, 201–205.

[33] S. W. Price, *The Old Masters of the Blue Grass,* Filson Club Publications, Number 17.

[34] *Autobiography of Peter Cartwright;* W. W. Sweet, *Circuit Rider Days in Indiana.*

[35] *Michigan Pioneer Collections,* III, 438; R. Babcock, *Memoir of Peck,* pp. 139–140.

[36] Between 1830 and 1845 most of the early laws regulating medical practice had been repealed. Improvement thereafter was by the profession and the schools. Robert Peter, *op. cit.,* pp. 49–55; Otto Juettner, "Rise of Medical Colleges in the Ohio Valley," *Ohio Arch. and Hist. Soc. Publications,* XXII, 481–491; L. H. Zeuch, *History of Medical Practice in Illinois,* pp. 183–238, 542–554; *Indiana Magazine of History,* XIX, 226–240 [Dr. John Evans]; G. H. W. Kemper, *A Medical*

History of Indiana, pp. 165–172; C. H. Rammelkamp, *Illinois College,* pp. 95–100; A. C. Cole, *The Era of the Civil War,* pp. 217–218.

[37] E. A. Miller, "The History of Educational Legislation in Ohio," *Ohio Arch. and Hist. Soc. Publications,* XXVII, 18–19, 64–68, 95–96; *ibid.,* XIV, 12–27; VI, 35–58; A. C. Cole, in *Ill. State Hist. Soc. Journal,* XIV, 317–318; XII, 264–270; *Indiana Magazine of History,* XII, 193–213.

[38] C. H. Rammelkamp, *op. cit.,* pp. 166–169, 156–158.

[39] United States Census, 1850.

[40] F. L. Mott, *A History of American Magazines,* pp. 384–390; *Wisconsin Magazine of History,* V, 43–56; VIII, 131–145; W. H. Venable, *op. cit.,* pp. 58–123, 267–296; *Indiana Magazine of History,* XX, 187–188; VIII, 181–186.

[41] S. W. Price, *op. cit.*

[42] Chas. Cist, *op. cit.,* pp. 121–128; A. T. Andreas, *History of Chicago,* p. 506.

[43] A. T. Andreas, *op. cit.,* pp. 496–500.

THE DEVELOPMENT OF CIVILIZATION
IN THE MIDDLE WEST, 1860–1900

JOHN D. HICKS

ABOUT 1900 years ago a wise man out of the East propounded the question: "Can any good thing come out of Nazareth?" Ever since that time, and probably also for much longer before, representatives of the older and more sophisticated centers of society have vented their scorn upon such crashers at the gates of civilization as have chanced to appear on any distant horizon. Recently the Spanish philosopher, Ortega y Gasset, in a series of circumlocutions so thoroughly involved as to make all other philosophers gasp with envy, has rung the changes upon this familiar theme. Europe, says Ortega, has nothing to learn from America, for American civilization is purely colonial and derivative, as empty as a hollow ball, and as totally lacking in that solid internal structure that makes European civilization a thing of beauty and a joy forever.[1]

Since Europeans have always found cause to look down upon Americans, it is not surprising that eastern Americans have also found cause to

[73]

look down upon western Americans. In 1787 Gouverneur Morris urged the federal convention to lay a heavy hand upon the privileges that new western states should enjoy in the union. "The proper school of political talents," he insisted, was to be found in "the busy haunts of men, not the remote wilderness. The back members are always averse to the best measures." [2] The advice of Morris went unheeded, and during the next hundred years the East, politically speaking, was sometimes trampled under foot. But the eastern sense of superiority was by no means daunted. Not only in political sagacity, but in every other respect also, the older parts of the country claimed a virtual monopoly on wisdom. Historians, readily conceding the point, found the origins of nearly everything significant in American history to the east of the Appalachians, if not, indeed, to the east of the Hudson.

And then, suddenly, a youthful historian out of the West, Frederick Jackson Turner of Wisconsin, a man who had seen with his own eyes the important rôle his section had played and was still playing in the life of the nation, turned the tables on the East. The West, he said, was the most American part of America, the frontier experience the most profound of all the influences that went into the shaping of the American character, what the

[74]

East was even now the West in no small part had determined, the East itself had once been West and had never quite been able to live the fact down. So dramatic was the Turner attack, so plausible his reasoning, so finished his rhetoric, that even the eastern historians were impressed. For nearly forty years the frontier hypothesis went almost unchallenged.[3]

But at last unmistakable rumblings from across the mountains are being heard. What did the West ever have, anyway, we are now asked, that it did not get from the East? How could the West have been civilized but for the work of patient missionaries bearing culture from the East? If the West has ever made any worth-while contribution to the history of the American people, does not the credit in the last analysis belong to the East, from which the West borrowed all its brightest ideas?[4] And the western school of historians, so long the proud proclaimers of a new and radical interpretation of American history, have not shown pronounced ability as defenders of what has now become sheer orthodoxy. For the most part they have only rephrased and reinterpreted the Turner arguments when, unless they had something different to offer, they might better have been content to repeat them. For what Turner had to say probably no one else will ever be able to say as well.

[75]

One hesitates to take his stand on middle ground, for to do so ensures that he will draw fire from both sides. And yet I can see no other solid ground upon which to stand. As a reasonably orthodox Turnerian I still see merit in the Turner contentions, especially when applied to the period which preceded the advance of the Industrial Revolution upon America. On the other hand, I feel that the striking changes which accompanied the opening of the industrial era have not yet received adequate attention from the western school of historians. Thanks to the easy means of communications which accompanied the new era, the West was opened to outside influences more freely than ever before; as freely, indeed, as was the East itself. Acted upon equally by the new forces there emerged both a new West and a new East, differing in some particulars, strangely alike in others, interdependent and complementary, neither to be regarded as merely the product of the other, both essential parts of an essentially new nation.

That the Middle West possesses a kind of sectional unity is sufficiently evident to obviate the necessity of arguing the case. Environmental conditions do not vary markedly from the Seven Ranges to the ninety-ninth meridian, nor from the Canadian border to the line of the Ohio River and the Missouri Compromise. The statements of a

[76]

habitants varied from nothing at all in some of the frontier states to twelve or thirteen per cent in the most populous.[6] The westward movement was still in progress, a fact which some of the older states of the section observed with some misgiving. "Movers" from the East, instead of halting in time to swell the census figures of some state on the left bank of the Mississippi, passed through the Old Northwest in a steady stream to the newer regions beyond. Moreover, all the older states of the Middle West saw a host of their own sons and daughters, native or adopted, caught up in the westward-moving stream. The restless, semi-vagrant wanderer, who was always uncomfortable when civilization began to press in upon him, could be spared; but there was also a steady drainage of fairly well-to-do citizens, who disposed of their property because they hoped that the dollars they would get for it would buy more acres of land, or bigger business opportunities, farther west. Sometimes these gamblers found that their judgment was wrong and their money was lost, but the migration continued just the same. Thus the whole region was still definitely in the formative stage. Like Mr. Roosevelt's dollar it had not yet reached the point of stabilization. Doubtless a substantial majority of its citizens had found permanent homes, but for a vast multitude any given portion

[78]

of the Middle West was still only a temporary abode, or a highway to some promised land.[7]

The chief concern of the inhabitants in a region so new is necessarily the exploitation of the natural resources that lie about them. Material things loom large in importance. The humble are busy acquiring homes, the far-sighted have their eyes open for unearned increment, the clever and the unscrupulous are on the scent of magnificent fortunes.[8] It is customary to assume that during this foundation-laying period the West lapsed into a sort of materialistic barbarism that precluded all attention to "those specializations and refinements which come from intelligently living together," if we may plagiarize Professor Fox's generous definition of civilization.[9] But there is good reason to believe that this early crudeness of the West has been much overstressed. Those of us who can remember our pioneer grandparents, or have verified the family traditions about them, find it hard to reconcile this notion of a startling lapse in civilization with many readily ascertainable facts. We do indeed recall well-authenticated tales of hard-working men and women who spent freely of their abundant energies in the conquest of new lands, the building of houses and barns, the struggle, sometimes successful, sometimes unavailing, to achieve the ordinary comforts of life. But we recall also tales of men who read

[79]

because of the enduring connections that bound it to the East, gained also. But nothing could be further from the truth than the assumption that the West was a heathen land which was converted to civilized ways only as a result of persistent propaganda emanating from the East.[11]

The most startling developments in the history of the later Middle West, as well as in the history of the nation and of the world, grew mainly out of the workings of the Industrial Revolution. By the end of the nineteenth century a Middle West has appeared that bears small resemblance either to the Middle West of 1860 or the East of 1860. The frontier line has been practically obliterated, and four new western states, Kansas, Nebraska, and the two Dakotas, have been admitted to the union. Fourteen cities of over one hundred thousand inhabitants have appeared to produce a further alteration of the landscape, while Chicago, the metropolis of the West, with a population of over a million and a half, has become the second city in the land. Towns have turned into small cities, and villages have turned into towns. In the most rural of the middle western states at least five per cent of the people now live in places of four thousand or more inhabitants, in some states forty or fifty per cent are so situated, and for the whole region over thirty-five per cent, measured by this standard, are city dwellers.[12] In less than four decades magnificent forests have been felled, rich mineral resources have been opened, railroads have extended their antennæ north, west, and south, agriculture has been mechanized, methods of marketing have been transformed, factories have been established, cities have acquired waterworks, sewer systems, electric lighting, paved streets and streetcars, homes have been filled with comforts and conveniences undreamed of in an earlier age, inventive genius has been fully unleashed.[13]

All this has happened, however, not because the West was west, but because the same thing was happening to the whole civilized world. The Middle West of 1900 has outgrown the East of 1860; it has more people, more wealth, more factories, more cities than the East of only forty years before. Not in the Middle West alone, but everywhere in the United States, the essentially rural culture that had become an American tradition is on the wane, and an industrial, city-led civilization is taking its place. The Middle West, like the American East and most of Western Europe, has gone in heavily for a new type of pioneering, industrial pioneering, and the days of the agricultural pioneer are numbered.[14] This new sort of pioneering is no east-to-west affair, but a steady advance all along the line. Perhaps the Middle West in the onward

[82]

march of industry occupies a kind of left flank position, but its leaders are abreast with those of the rest of the world, and sometimes they forge a little ahead. At Minneapolis in the 1870's, American ingenuity, borrowing what it could from Europe, particularly Hungary, and inventing when it had to, worked out the "patent" process of manufacturing flour that was soon to revolutionize the industry throughout the world.[15] At Milwaukee, in 1868, a journalist and prominent state politician named C. Latham Sholes invented the typewriter.[16] An Oberlin professor, Charles M. Hall, some years later discovered a commercially profitable means of producing aluminum.[17] And what shall we say of such other Middle Westerners as James B. Eads, Thomas A. Edison, Henry Ford, Wilbur and Orville Wright? [18]

It is hard to reconcile with these revolutionary circumstances the theory that civilization has been transmitted to the West without essential modification through the agency of conscious cultural carriers from the East. If, as seems reasonable, our definition of civilization is to be construed as including materialistic progress as well as that which for lack of a better term we call spiritual, then the Middle West seems to have done its part. But from any point of view the Middle West has become, well before the end of the nineteenth century, one of the component parts of a new and rapidly developing America rather than a colony of the older East. Professor Fox's four stages for the "transit" of civilization from an old region to a new one may serve well enough as an eighteenth-century bridge across the Atlantic, but when applied to the Middle West of the later nineteenth century these several stages tend completely to merge. So much smaller has the world become, so much more closely knit by the new means of communication, that foreign practitioners of practically every known specialty are at all times freely entering the Middle West; middle western youth are going in a steady stream to eastern centers and to Europe "to attend upon instruction"; middle western institutions of a wide variety of special learnings are being established, with more or less dependence on outside centers for their teachers; and yet, in a constantly increasing number, middle western institutions are able to maintain themselves with no appreciably greater amount of borrowing from the outside than they are able to lend in return.[19] Particularly do the western cities come to possess nearly everything, good or bad, that can be found anywhere else, and the really significant transit of civilization that goes on is less an east-to-west affair than a city-to-country affair.

It would be idle to argue that the Middle West

owes nothing to the East or to the rest of the world, and no such argument is intended. Rather, it is the close connection between East and West, the interdependence of Europe and America, the easy give-and-take made possible by the new world order that seems so significant. The Middle West takes on a personality of its own, in part by picking up from here and there the ideas it likes, in part by independent experiences and experiments from which it acquires something to hand back to the older centers of civilization in return for what it has received.

It may be worth while to pause at this point in order to take cognizance of the fact that American historians, with myself as a horrible example, have been accused of writing history in a vacuum, of ignoring the fact that conditions outside the United States have at all times affected the life of the American people.[20] There is some justice to the charge. Stricken with the same blindness that afflicts our diplomatic isolationists, we have kept our eyes so tightly glued upon our own development that we have sometimes forgotten that its mainsprings were not invariably to be found within our borders. The rôle of the immigrant in the making of latter-day America has received, thanks to the work of such men as Professors Hansen and Blegen,[21] increasingly adequate attention, but the repercussions in the United States of European, Latin American, and perhaps also Asiatic, developments are still too frequently overlooked. The destiny of the United States is, after all, intimately related to the destiny of the rest of the nations of the world; whenever anything of significance happens in one quarter of the globe it is certain to awaken echoes in all the other quarters. A world war and a world depression have made us acutely aware of this situation for the moment, and we are not surprised to note the borrowings back and forth of the various "new deals" by which recovery is being vouchsafed. We may well review our whole history in the light generated by the present emergency. And, parenthetically, our writers of European history may well take off the blinders by which they have long so proudly protected themselves from observing that the development of modern Europe has been affected, perchance, by happenings on this side of the Atlantic; even, indeed, by happenings on this side of the Appalachians.

In adjusting itself socially to the new conditions brought on by the Industrial Revolution the United States, East as well as West, tended often to follow strictly European leads. Thanks in no small part to the "safety-valve" of the frontier, these problems were hardly as pressing in America as in Europe, but as fast as they appeared European experience was drawn upon freely in an effort to find satisfactory solutions. Many early American trades unions, for example, were frankly imitative of similar organizations in Europe, and in the Middle West labor organizations were long confined almost exclusively to immigrant groups who brought their ideas directly from Europe. The doctrines of the Chicago anarchists, whose activities so excited Americans of the '80's, were imported ready made, as were also the more moderate theories held by the disciples of Karl Marx.[22] The various types of social legislation advocated in America were with great frequency of European origin. Nor did these notions invariably advance by easy stages, east to west. They appeared in America whenever and wherever conditions were ripe for their appearance, and the opposition not too pronounced. The devotion of the frontier Populists to the rights of labor should not be ignored,[23] the flirtations of middle western Wisconsin with European concepts of the function of the state must needs be considered,[24] and the foundation of Hull House in Chicago by a young woman who got her ideas directly from London rather than from New York is a plain case in point.[25]

That the West had various contributions of its own to make can also be successfully maintained.

[87]

No better example can be cited, perhaps, than the doctrine of railway rate regulation generally associated with the Granger movement. The railroads, new to the West, but relatively new also the whole country over, had only one rule for fixing rates, and that they applied with indifferent skill. They meant to charge all the traffic would bear. The burden their rates placed upon the land-locked Middle West soon became intolerable, but the orthodox method for abating this evil was to encourage competition. The Illinois constitutional convention which met in the winter of 1869–1870 was inclined at first so to maintain. Easier terms for the railway promoters and more generous inducements to investors would turn the trick. But toward the end of the session a Bloomington lawyer, Reuben M. Benjamin, arrested the attention of the delegates in a well devised argument to the effect that the "power to limit the rates of charges of common carriers as the public good may require is a governmental power which no legislature can irrevocably abandon or bargain away to any individual or corporation." [26] At first blush such unbelievable heresy seemed scarcely to warrant attention, and yet the advantages that might flow from its adoption were not to be despised. At length Benjamin talked the convention around, and the Granger doctrine of rate regulation, a direct

[88]

eastern states, less afflicted by railway extortions than the West, rejected or ignored. This, it would seem, is not an instance of the advance of civilization from somewhere else into the West, but of the advance of civilization within the West itself.

All too little time remains in which to multiply illustrations, but the development of educational facilities in the Middle West during the period under discussion must certainly not be ignored. In this respect the Middle West kept well abreast of the East, maintained close contact with Europe, and blazed some new trails. Thanks to the terms of the Northwest Ordinance the urge for a free public school system was a birthright in every western state; and in no other section of the nation was faith in general education as a remedy for the ills that afflicted mankind more pronounced. On this point the foreign element, especially the Germans and the Scandinavians, who had been used to liberal educational opportunities in their homelands, agreed heartily with the native Americans.[29] Democracy in education may not have been the panacea that our forefathers believed it to be, but the fact remains that by the end of the century the states of the Middle West had achieved a higher percentage of literates among their people than most of the states of the East. Sometimes innovations, such, for example, as kindergartens and man-

[90]

ual training courses, came to the Middle West directly from abroad.[30] Public high schools were not precisely novelties, East or West, but in the middle western states the opportunities they offered were made available to the masses with all possible speed. The accrediting of high schools, which was first introduced by the University of Michigan as a device for raising the high school level of instruction, became immediately popular and was widely copied.[31]

In the realm of higher education the state university wrested leadership from the small denominational college and pushed forward with tremendous speed the doctrine of practicality in education, a doctrine often preached but less frequently practiced in the East. The system of free electives, inaugurated by Harvard, was quickly pressed into service, curriculums were broadened to make possible a college education for students who had no knowledge of Latin or Greek, numerous subsidiary colleges, such as pharmacy, engineering, forestry, and most especially agriculture, were introduced, through coeducation the same educational privileges that were given to men were made available to women, and through extension courses a sincere effort was made to give some of the advantages of a college education to those who might not hope to live within college walls.[32]

[91]

Graduate study as a part of the American educational system long lagged behind, and for many years eastern as well as western universities submitted without resentment to the necessity of sending their students abroad, usually to Germany, for advanced training.[33] But the establishment of graduate schools at Hopkins and Harvard soon led to emulation by the western state universities, and the situation was still further altered when John D. Rockefeller, an Ohio industrialist, provided the means for William R. Harper, of Ohio birth, to create the University of Chicago. Before long this great middle western university, full-grown from its birth, began to turn out a yearly crop of Ph.D.'s, trained in nearly every known discipline, that rivaled in size and quality the output of even the oldest and largest of the eastern universities.[34] The day was done when the middle western student had of necessity to go to the East or to Europe to break into the fraternity of scholars. Many, of course, did go east, or to Europe, but easterners, an occasional European, and a flock of Asiatics also found their way to the Middle West. Western professors made serious contributions to their specialties, and with increasing frequency they were called to chairs in eastern universities. In 1893, for example, Turner of Wisconsin propounded his frontier hypothesis and began to train the school of historians whose point of view was so soon to be generally accepted, only to be called presently to Harvard as a needed antidote, perhaps, to the growing provincialism of American history as presented in that eastern center of learning.

One more illustration of the western contribution to civilization must suffice. Creative writing, to borrow a none too lovely term from our departments of literature, seems to be somehow associated with the highest good, and by the last half of the nineteenth century Middle Westerners had reached even this coveted goal. Now the birth of a literary genius is not a matter of transit across the Atlantic or across the Appalachians, nor of the advance of civilization from one place to another. It may happen any time, anywhere. Possibly genius may be suppressed by unfavorable surroundings, and conditions of life in the early Middle West may so have operated. Abraham Lincoln, however, grew out of these primitive conditions, and only a few critics would deny him a place among the masters of English prose. Two decades after Lincoln assumed the presidency, Englishmen were according recognition to another western writer, Mark Twain, and a little later even New Englanders conceded with some reluctance that at last books worth reading were being written by a man who came out of the West. It is indeed hard to see how a writer could have been more closely associated with his environment than the author of *Life on the Mississippi* and the *Innocents*. Mark Twain was educated, as were so many other Middle Westerners of his time, primarily in the school of experience, he wrote of the life which surrounded him, and yet few, if any, American writers of his generation deserve to be set above him.[35] From his time forward the West continued to produce writers of merit. William Dean Howells, whose Ohio birth and training he at least did not forget, stood far more consciously than Mark Twain, and perhaps with greater sophistication, for the same sort of realism, the same insistence on truth in fiction. Hamlin Garland, too, came out of the West, and although he, like Howells, owed much to the East as well as to the West, his youthful experiences gave him the materials with which to work, and possibly the inspiration to write. The list need not be prolonged, as it could be so easily, especially if writers of the twentieth century were included. The literature which has come out of the West in these later years may not be prophetic of a new Shakespearean age, but on the whole the West gives about as good as it gets.

In many respects the development of civilization in the East and in the West proceeded side by side and was shaped after a common pattern. Educational institutions themselves, which tended increasingly to become alike the whole country over, had a part in the promotion of this standardization of American tastes, habits, and opinions. The Chautauqua movement, which began as a summer encampment on the shores of Lake Chautauqua, New York, for the training of Sunday school teachers, but soon widened its scope and spread to nearly every cross-roads village in the land, provided a tremendous avenue for the nation-wide circulation of everything that purchasable "talent" had to offer. Newspapers, whether they boasted merely of presenting "all the news that's fit to print," or disdaining such subtleties, claimed outright a position as the "world's greatest," strikingly resembled one another, not only in the news they supplied but also in their advertisements, their special "services," their Sunday supplements. Magazines with an all-American circulation spread identical views. Philanthropists in each sizable center found soul-easement in the endowment of hospitals, libraries, museums, art galleries, observatories, and occasionally even symphony orchestras and grand opera companies; while one of the most ambitious of their number, Andrew Carnegie, bent on the widest possible dispersion of his vast fortune, began to build, east, west, north, and south, what the irreverent sometimes called his "fire-escapes." Nor may we overlook the standardizing influences of the Phila-

[95]

in the Middle West of the Civil War period, was never wholly shattered by the impact of the Industrial Revolution, and some of the frontier ideals were reinforced rather than reversed in the new age. If the pioneer's belief in individual freedom was soon shown to be out of harmony with his insistence on democracy, there were many who refused to recognize the fact, and many also who pinned their faith to the one ideal or the other. Moreover the pioneer's love of conquest, his optimistic outlook on life, his willingness to accept innovations formed a social inheritance that it was not easy to forget.

Possibly the most distinctive qualities of the Middle West proceed from this newness, this youthful lack of sophistication, which of all things American our Spanish philosopher, Ortega, most deplores. The Middle West has not yet grown cynical; it can still believe; it has not lost hope. For its self-appointed leaders—Rotarians, Women's Clubbers, Uplifters, Sons of the Wild Jackass all—civilization is not yet exhausted; life still holds something in store. Perhaps we of the West are only children who believe in Santa Claus; but perhaps western faith will help to remove our current mountains of depression, perhaps western belief that the disorders of the world can yet be righted will help to right them, perhaps even the naïve

[97]

western assumption that the American experiment in democracy cannot possibly fail will help to keep it from failing.

[1] José Ortega y Gasset, "Ueber die Vereinigten Staaten," *Reichsausgabe der Frankfurter Zeitung,* June 20, 1933. Aus dem Juni-Heft der *Europaischen Revue* (Berlin).

[2] *The Records of the Federal Convention of 1787,* Max Farrand, ed. (New Haven, 1911), I, 583.

[3] Carl L. Becker, "Frederick Jackson Turner," in *American Masters of Social Science,* H. W. Odum, ed. (New York, 1927), pp. 273–318.

[4] The posthumous appearance of Turner's *The Significance of Sections in American History* (New York, 1933) gave an excellent opportunity for reviewers to state their opinions on Turner's contribution to the interpretation of American history. With this book as his text Benjamin F. Wright, Jr., in the *New England Quarterly,* VI, 630–634, (Sept., 1933) repeated criticisms he had previously made in an article, "American Democracy and the Frontier," *Yale Review,* XX, 349–365 (Dec., 1930). The Marxian objections were voiced by Louis M. Hacker, "Sections—or Classes," in the *Nation,* CXXXVII, 108–110 (July 26, 1933), with significant modifications suggested by Benjamin Stolberg, "Turner, Marx, and the A. F. of L.," in the *Nation,* CXXXVII, 302–303 (Sept. 13, 1933). F. L. Paxson, "A Generation of the Frontier Hypothesis, 1893–1932," *Pacific Historical Review,* II, 34–51 (Mar., 1933), offered some amendments to Turner's principal generalizations, which Joseph Schafer, "Turner's Frontier Philosophy," *Wisconsin Magazine of History,* XVI, 451–469 (June, 1933), brilliantly rejected. For further illuminating comment from Dr. Schafer's pen see "Turner's America," *Wisconsin Magazine of History,* XVII, 445–465 (June, 1934).

[5] Emilius O. Randall and Daniel J. Ryan, *History of Ohio* (New York, 1912), V, 4.

[98]

[6] *Twelfth Census of the United States, 1900* (Washington, 1903), I, 430–433 and plate no. 9. See also *Statistical Atlas*, plate no. 9.

[7] *Eighth Census of the United States, 1860* (Washington, 1864), pp. xxxiii–xxxv, on "Internal Migration." See also *Twelfth Census*, I, cxlvii.

[8] This idea has never been better developed than by E. L. Godkin in his essay on "Aristocratic Opinions of Democracy," *North American Review*, C, 194–232 (Jan., 1865).

[9] Dixon Ryan Fox, "Civilization in Transit," *American Historical Review*, XXXII, 753 (July, 1927). Cf. Suzanne La Follette, *Art in America* (New York, 1929), pp. 110–111.

[10] The biographies of middle western pioneers, as presented in the *Dictionary of American Biography*, throw much light on this subject.

[11] John C. Parish, "The Persistence of the Westward Movement," *Yale Review*, XV, 471–477 (Jan., 1926).

[12] *Twelfth Census of the United States*, I, lxxxiv, 430–433, plate no. 9, and *Statistical Atlas*, plate no. 13.

[13] A. M. Schlesinger, *The Rise of the City* (New York, 1933), chs. 3, 4.

[14] Cf. Charles A. Beard and Mary R. Beard, *The Rise of American Civilization* (New York, 1927), II, 188–210, on the "Triumph of Business Enterprise."

[15] Frederick Merk, *Economic History of Wisconsin* (Madison, 1916), pp. 138–140.

[16] *Ibid.*, pp. 155–157.

[17] Harvey O'Connor, *Mellon's Millions* (New York, 1933), p. 80.

[18] Turner, *Significance of Sections*, ch. 10, on "The Children of the Pioneers"; Dumas Malone, "The Geography of American Achievement," *Atlantic Monthly*, CXLIV, 669–679 (Dec., 1934).

[19] Fox, in *American Historical Review*, XXXII, 754.

[20] James C. Malin, "Notes on the Literature of Populism," *Kansas Historical Quarterly*, I, 160–164 (Feb., 1932).

[21] Marcus L. Hansen, *German Schemes of Colonization before 1860* (Northampton, Mass., 1924) ; Theodore C. Blegen, *Norwegian Migration to America, 1825–1860* (Northfield, Minn., 1931). See also Laurence M. Larson, "The Norwegian Element in the Northwest," *American Historical Review*, XL, 69–81 (Oct., 1934).

[22] Merk, *Economic History of Wisconsin*, pp. 170–172; E. L. Bogart and C. M. Thompson, *The Industrial State, 1870–1893, The Centennial History of Illinois* (Springfield, 1920), IV, 51, 439–443, 461–464.

[23] See, for example, the Omaha platform of 1892, in Edward Stanwood, *A History of the Presidency* (Boston, 1898), I, 509–513.

[24] C. C. McCarthy, *The Wisconsin Idea* (New York, 1912), pp. 10–11, 28–30.

[25] Jane Addams, *Twenty Years at Hull House* (New York, 1910), chs. 4, 5.

[26] *Debates and Proceedings of the Constitutional Convention of the State of Illinois, Convened at the City of Springfield, Tuesday, Dec. 13, 1869* (Springfield, 1870), II, 1641–1643.

[27] *The Bench and Bar of Illinois*, John M. Palmer, ed. (Chicago, 1899), II, 727–734.

[28] Allan Nevins, *The Emergence of Modern America* (New York, 1927), pp. 161–163.

[29] Schlesinger, *Rise of the City*, p. 170.

[30] J. P. Dunn, *History of Indianapolis* (Chicago, 1910), I, 276. Reuben Gold Thwaites and others, *Wisconsin in Three Centuries* (New York, 1906), IV, 174–175 .

[31] Conrad E. Patzer, *Public Education in Wisconsin* (Madison, 1924), ch. 12; Schlesinger, *Rise of the City*, p. 204.

[32] W. R. Harper, *The Trend in Higher Education* (New York, 1897), chs. 6, 7.

[33] C. F. Thwing, *The American and the German University* (New York, 1928), p. 42.

[34] Bogart and Thompson, *Centennial History*, IV, 215–216;

T. W. Goodspeed, *William Rainey Harper* (Chicago, 1928).
[35] Bernard A. De Voto, *Mark Twain's America* (Boston, 1932), p. 321.
[36] Becker, in *American Masters of Social Science,* p. 300.

REMARKS

MARCUS L. HANSEN

As I have listened to the reading of the papers this evening I have referred occasionally to the printed program and have noted with some interest that the topic scheduled for the session is "The Advance of Civilization into the Middle West." Civilization is usually interpreted to include everything that one desires to talk about, and therefore the concentration upon the "Turner hypothesis" is a matter worthy of note. I shall not attempt in the ten minutes allotted me to discuss everything else; but, rather, if there is a good fight going on, I hasten to join the combatants on the bloody sands.

Professor Wright is to be congratulated upon the temerity with which he has invaded the historians' shrine and challenged their most sacred dogma. We have had it coming to us. Forty years ago the frontier interpretation of American history was propounded. In the four decades that followed, how productive historical scholarship has been! Hundreds of dissertations, literally scores of journals, month after month, quarter after quarter, pouring out their factual contributions. But not an-

[103]

other new interpretation among them! The majority of scholars, I fear, had no interest in interpretations; there were too many documents to be digested. But then, when called upon for a theory, they gave the first that popped into their minds; and by repetition they unconsciously committed themselves thereto.

Especially is this true in some of the older universities and colleges of the country. There, above all, pure, unadulterated "Turnerism" is being taught. Those who never saw a frontier are most enthusiastic in their explanation of its mission. It is a President whose whole career has been lived far remote from the pioneer West who, in his addresses and papers, has adopted the Turner "free land" theory as the historical basis of his New Deal philosophy.

But in the Middle West, the region from which the prophet came, a home-town skepticism is revealing itself. You have this evening heard Professor Hicks, who occupies, I believe, the professorial chair from which Mr. Turner made his most significant pronouncements, express a desire to be a middle-of-the-roader. Many obscure articles and many unpublished theses in western universities are presenting a mass of factual evidence which, if boiled down into theory, could be organized into

The situation is somewhat similar to that which faced foreign immigrants into the Middle West. Because we have all heard of Carl Schurz and the Chicago anarchists, we assume that all immigrants were either liberals or radicals. But they weren't. I believe that for every liberal there were ten conservatives among them. They emigrated, in fact, because they were conservatives—conservatives being those that have something to conserve. They wanted to conserve their religion, or their property, or their standing in society. They believed that under American institutions they could so do. To change those institutions was not their intention. We all know that the Irish, Germans, Swedes, and Norwegians of the 1850's affiliated with the Democratic Party. But this came about, not, as is usually said, because the Democratic Party wooed them the more ardently, but because they wanted to be won. The Democratic Party was the conservative party of the day; therefore, they became Democrats. But that was for a few years only. On the frontier they underwent a typical western evolution. In a few years they had gone liberal and become Republicans. I might illustrate the same tendency in the experiences of their successors after the Civil War. From being conservative Republicans they turned into Populists, Greenbackers, and Farm-Laborites.

Native-born and foreign-born, alike, experienced a rapid change in sentiments. But this change is reflected not so much in state machinery as in the national politics that concerned them the most: land, improvements, finances, Indians.

To the second of Professor Wright's charges I have a more serious objection. I question one of the premises on which he has worked: his interpretation of the Turner doctrine. Neither from my reading, nor from Professor Turner's classes and seminars, did I ever get the idea that the influence of the West was exerted through imitation. That is, that the State of Illinois, let us say, liberalized the franchise; therefore, Massachusetts said, "That is a good idea; let us do the same." It wasn't what Illinois *did* but what it *was* that counted. That is what Turner taught. The free lands of the West, the richer opportunities that it offered attracted those whom the East did not want to lose, and they aroused discontent. So in an attempt to hold some and satisfy others reform was brought about. As a result it is quite possible that eastern legislation on these matters should precede western. Moreover, legal restraints must be read in the light of opportunity. A property qualification on voting or holding office was a far heavier burden in the East than in the West, where the acquisition of property was more readily achieved. I admit that the progress of reform in the East, its origins, its supporters, its arguments, must be subjected to much more investigation before we can judge fairly. But I will not concede that the listing of dates is any serious attack upon the frontier doctrine.

And now some one will ask the question, "What is this Neo-Turnerism that you were talking about?" Briefly, it is propounded by those who believe that the West was not merely the frontier of the American population, but of the European population as well. Professor Hicks has pointed out that social theories and educational practices that became distinctly middle western were imported from Europe. Such ideas, brought from across the Atlantic, were probably much more tenacious than those that came from the American East. I cannot enlarge upon the religious, linguistic, and other reasons for this tenacity; but it was a vital fact in the shaping of popular sentiment. When the Turner hypothesis is modified, I believe that it is in the recognition of this fact that the change will come. Our primary task, therefore, lies in the appraisal of these forces.

Here there arises a great obstacle. We know so little of what the foreigner brought with him. We know so little of the social environment from which he came. American social history cannot be written until the social history of modern Europe has been written; and that has not been done.

[108]

And so, gentlemen, I think that we would feel better if, instead of quarreling among ourselves, we should turn and face our common enemy, many of whom I see down in the trenches before us this evening. I refer to our friends, the Americans engaged in the research and writing of European history. They haven't done right by us. They haven't told us what we want to know or what we ought to know. Every fall undergraduates pass through my office and I check over their study-lists. To many I must say, "In history, you are taking nothing but American; why not some European?" Their question is "Why?" To which I must reply, "To get the background of American history." And yet I know that the background that they will get will be one that confuses instead of clarifies. The two pictures are drawn on different scales and in different shades. When one is put upon the other, the result is confusion. When we draw up the Historians' Code let us base it upon the theory of the Agricultural Adjustment Act. For one year take all scholars in American history out of production and, at the same time, all scholars in European history. Then we will probably do what is not unknown among the farmers. If forbidden to plant corn, they plant wheat or cotton. Thus, all the scholars in American history will study European, and all the scholars in European history will study American. As a result, we will learn more about European history and more about American history than we have for many a year; and—what is most important—the parts will fit.

A century ago, biology was mainly descriptive as history is to-day. Then a naturalist named Charles Darwin took a trip around the world and studied animal forms in every continent he visited. It was from comparison that Charles Darwin drew the principles on which the doctrine of evolution was based—and the million facts of the animal world had an interpretation. A student of literature in Copenhagen, Georg Brandes, devoted himself to the investigation not of Danish writers but of the writers of the western nations. His *Main Streams in the Literature of the Nineteenth Century* made more understandable the cultural development of each separate nation. We have comparative zoology, comparative literature, comparative law, comparative religion. When are we going to have comparative social history? When we do, we can answer the questions: what parts of middle western civilization came from abroad? what parts from the East? what arose from the native soil? Only when that is done can we fully appraise the historical theories of F. J. Turner.

[110]